Daisy Doe

Written and Illustrated by

Sandra Tate

Copyright© 2025
All Rights Reserved
ISBN: 979-8-9925820-6-2

Daisy is a mother deer
with two spotted fawns in tow.
Freckles is a baby buck.
Speckles is a baby doe.

In the spring, the fawns are born,
sometimes it's two or three!
Right after birth, they stand up
and take steps carefully.

When Daisy goes to look for food,
she can be away for hours.
She hides her fawns in separate spots
for added safety measures.

For weeks they both stay hidden.
They lay low when Mom's away.
Their spots help make them hard to see,
which keeps them safe throughout the day.

In the fall, deer like to eat acorns, nuts, and corn. In winter, they eat buds and twigs, and green plants when it's warm.

They eat breakfast every morning. They have quite the appetite! They eat a snack late afternoon, and then again at night.

For ten weeks she nurses them,
which is not very long.
She feeds them five times every day.
By four months, their spots are gone!

At five weeks old they follow her
to learn to look for food.
Males leave their mom at just one year.
Females leave after two!

Growing fawns run and jump
because they love to play.
They make new friends with others
as they go throughout their day!

Sneaky Squirrel, Fancy Fox,
and Ringo Raccoon
like playing in the forest,
because they live there, too!

Daisy is a white-tailed deer.
She weighs 100 pounds!
A male is called a buck or stag
and weighs 150 pounds!

Deer hear and see things really well
and run 30 miles per hour!
They can jump up eight feet high
and also swim with power!

Grunt, snort, bleat, and stomp
are some of their many sounds.
They also often leave a scent
to say, "Hey! I am in town!"

When a white-tailed deer becomes afraid,
its tail stands up and starts to wave!
It's like a flag that's snowy white,
warning every deer in sight!

A buck grows antlers on his head.
They are also called a rack.
He sheds them in the winter.
In the spring, they will grow back!

When it's time to lose his antlers,
it does not hurt the deer.
If one falls off and one does not,
he'll look really weird!

Deer are very shy and scared.
They don't like to hang around.
They have large eyes to see
and big ears to hear each sound.

So, if you see Miss Daisy Doe
with her young fawns having fun,
be very still and quiet,
or they will surely run!

Sandra Tate is a piano teacher in Spicewood, Texas. She and her husband, David, have two married children, Joshua and Jennifer. Her hobbies include drawing, painting, and photography. She enjoys taking pictures of the wildlife in her very own backyard. That's why she calls them Nosy Neighbors! David and Sandra provide food and water for the deer, foxes, raccoons, squirrels, jackrabbits, and birds to make sure they make regular visits! Daisy Doe loves to eat the bird seeds that fall on the ground! Sandra wrote this story in 2021 during the pandemic which altered the lives of humans, but did not seem to impact the curiosity of the Nosy Neighbors!

www.ingramcontent.com/pod-product-compliance
Lightning Source LLC
Chambersburg PA
CBRC091142030426
42337CB00010B/77